For Mary Whitehouse, who took me to Hawai'i and
called me Family before I was — B. M. J.

For Fannie, forever and for always beautiful — B. L.

The author gratefully acknowledges the help of
Ka'ōhua Lucas, whose sensitivity and knowledge
helped make this a better book.

Text © 2008 by Barbara M. Joosse.
Illustrations © 2008 by Barbara Lavallee.
All rights reserved.

Typeset in Goudy.
The illustrations in this book were rendered in watercolor.
Manufactured in Hong Kong.

Library of Congress Cataloging-in-Publication Data
Joosse, Barbara M.
Grandma calls me Beautiful / by Barbara Joosse ; illustrated by Barbara Lavallee.
p. cm.
Summary: A Hawaiian grandmother tells her granddaughter a favorite story about how much she loves her.
Includes a glossary with definitions and explanations of Hawaiian words and customs.
ISBN 978-0-8118-5815-1
[1. Grandmothers—Fiction. 2. Storytelling—Fiction. 3. Hawaii—Fiction.] I. Lavallee, Barbara, ill. II. Title.
PZ7.J7435Gr 2008
[E]—dc22
2007028240

10 9 8 7 6 5 4 3 2 1

Chronicle Books LLC
680 Second Street, San Francisco, California 94107

www.chroniclekids.com

Grandma Calls Me Beautiful

by Barbara M. Joosse   illustrated by Barbara Lavallee

chronicle books · san francisco

"Open your eyes," said the grandmother,
"so I can see who you are."

The baby opened her eyes,
and the grandmother looked inside.

"Aloha!" she said.
"You're bright as a kukui torch.
Your breath is sweet as breadfruit pudding,
and your skin is soft as kapa cloth.

"I will call you Beautiful,
because you are."

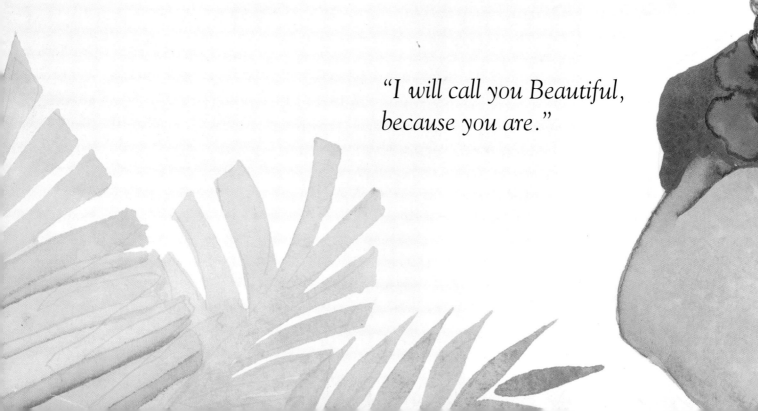

Once upon an island
in the deep blue sea . . .
a new girl-baby was born.

"That was me," said Beautiful.
"I was the girl-baby."
        "So you were," said Grandma, smiling.

"Tūtū? Tell me our story." Beautiful
made herself small as a kalo sprout,
and nestled against Grandma's side.

"A story? But there are so many.
Which one will I choose?"

"You know, Tūtū! *Our* story.
The Beautiful one."

Grandma picked up a string
and began . . .

As Grandma wove the rest of the talk-story, Beautiful's fingers twitched along.

The village sang to Beautiful:
Aunties beat the kapa cloth, tap tap tap.
Papas kneaded the soil, pat pat pat.
And spotted dogs barked at the
noonday sun, woof!

The sea danced for Beautiful:
  Seaweed swayed to the rhythm of the waves,
    while fish twirled through holes
      in the bright coral reef.

At last, the grandmother touched
noses with Beautiful so she could
share her breath.

Then she held her upside down
so she could walk on the sky.

Finished, Grandma tucked
the string away.

"Tūtū," said Beautiful. "The chickens
have fancy-feather colors."
        "'Ae! They're puffed up with color."

"And the piglets and dragonflies and
birds! Even the land snails are like
jewels in the trees."
        "Yes, they sing about their color."

"But my hair is plain black."
    "Black is the color of the deep, dark night,
    snapping with stars."

"And my skin is brown."
    "Brown is the color of a kalo field
    kneaded smooth by many feet."

"Tūtū, am I still beautiful?"
        "Beautiful is who you are."

"What if I grew big?"
        "Then you'd be Big-Beautiful."

"What if I grew very, very big,
and you grew very, very small,
and I sat on your lap and
squashed you flat?"

"Then I'd squeeeeeze myself out,
and sit on your lap."

"Sometimes Mama says I have
minnows squirming under my skin."

"Then you're wiggly,
but you're still Beautiful."

"Sometimes I scare Rooster,
just to hear his big noise."

"Then you're a little bit naughty,
but still, you're Beautiful."

Beautiful uncurled the fingers of Grandma's hand
and kissed the soft inside.

"Aloha, aloha, Beautiful!"
Grandma sang.

"You're the song of the village
and dance of the deep blue sea.
Part of the mamas and the papas,
and the dear little babies and me.

You are who you are—
bright as a kukui torch,
sweet as breadfruit pudding,
soft as kapa cloth.

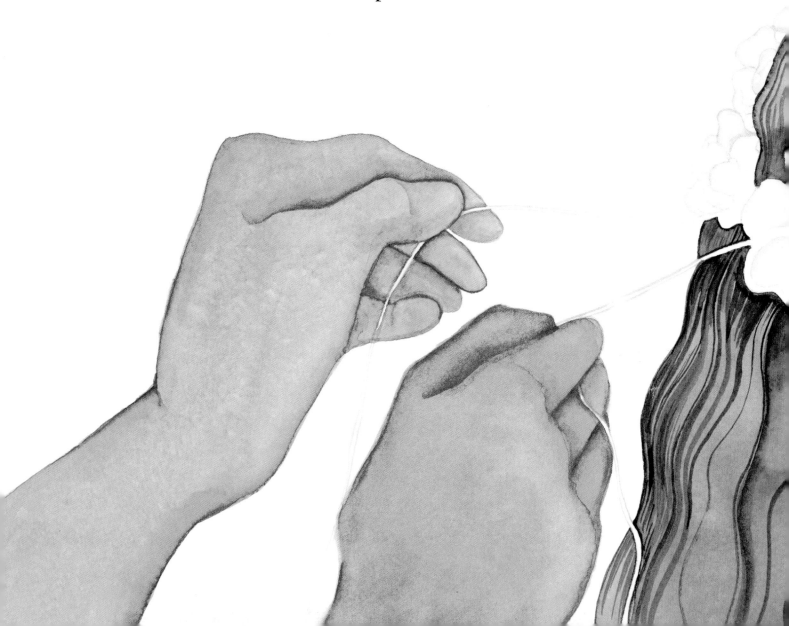

Forever
and for always,
Beautiful."

Glossary

Grandma and Beautiful live in Hawai'i. Like most native Hawaiians, they live in a way that's mostly-modern and partly-ancient. Grandma likes to tell Beautiful's favorite story both because it's a way for her to let Beautiful know she's special and because it reminds her of the traditions of her long-ago family and the island that is her home.

In this glossary you'll find additional information about some of the Hawaiian words and traditions featured in this book. Before 1820, the Hawaiian language was only spoken. Then American missionaries assigned the Hawaiian language just eight consonants, eliminating many letter sounds the Hawaiians used. That's the reason you'll find some Hawaiian words spelled different ways. The Hawaiian words below are spelled in the traditional way.

'AE (pronounced ah-eh) Yes!

ALOHA This word means many things to Hawaiians, including hello, good-bye, love, and kindness.

BREADFRUIT (*'ulu*, pronounced oo-loo) *'Ulu* was a common food for early Hawaiians. It was broiled or baked and also made into breadfruit pudding (*pepeie'e*, pronounced peh-peh-ee-eh-eh). Here's how to make breadfruit pudding: Mash ripe breadfruit, mix with coconut cream, then wrap in ti-leaf bundles and steam.

HEI (pronounced heh-ee) *Hei* is a string design woven with your fingers—like the familiar "cat's cradle." Both the string and the graceful "dance of your hands" as you weave help illustrate a story. Some *hei* are simple and some are very difficult.

KALO (pronounced kah-loh) *Kalo* fields were located just outside the villages in specially constructed ponds (*lo'i*, pronounced loh-ee). Native Hawaiians believe they're direct descendants from the *kalo* plant and they name parts of the family after parts of the plant (parent = *makua* = main plant; child = *'oha* = sprout).

KAPA (pronounced kah-pah) Long-ago Hawaiians were known for very soft *kapa* cloth. Only women were allowed to make *kapa*, which they did in special work houses (*hale kuku*, pronounced hah-leh koo-koo). In every village, the tap-tap-tap of their work was a familiar sound, reassuring as the beat of a heart. It has been said that women could tell secrets to each other in the rhythm of their beating.

KAPU (pronounced kah-poo) There were many *kapus* (laws) that told early Hawaiians what they could—and could not!—do. Most *kapu* protected the energy power (*mana*, pronounced mah-nah) of people, the land, and the sea. It was *kapu* for women to cook. Men's and women's food were cooked in separate outdoor ovens. It was also *kapu* for men and women to eat together.

KUKUI (pronounced koo-koo-ee) The oil from the *kukui* nut can be burned in a torch or used for healing.

LAND SNAILS In Hawai'i, land snails are so colorful they're sometimes called "tree jewels." And they really do sing!

TALK-STORY An informal conversation. Like a picture book, a talk-story is sometimes illustrated with song, *hei*, or dance, like the hula.

TOUCHING NOSES Native Hawaiians believe that sharing breath (*ha*) is a very loving thing to do. They do this by pressing their foreheads together and gently touching noses.

TŪTŪ (Grandma, pronounced too-too) Long-ago Hawaiians took special pleasure in raising their grandchildren—it was their job and their joy. Even though Beautiful's grandmother is modern, she still feels the same way.

Here's a hei (string design) you can make.

Honu (Turtle)

This design is easiest and most fun when you have a friend or family member to help you.

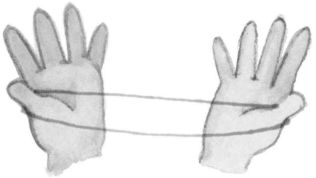

1. Start with about 5 feet of string or yarn. Tie the ends together to make a big circle.

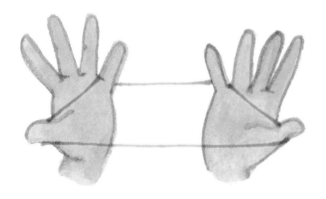

2. Loop the string around your thumbs and pinkie fingers so that the string crosses your palms. With your fingers spread wide and your palms facing each other, pull your hands apart until the string is tight.

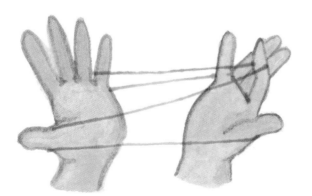

3. Slide your *right* index finger under the string that crosses your *left* palm.
4. Then slide your *left* index finger under the string that crosses your *right* palm. Pull the string tight again.

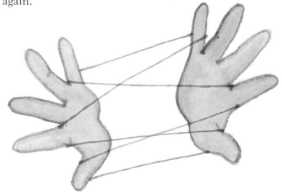

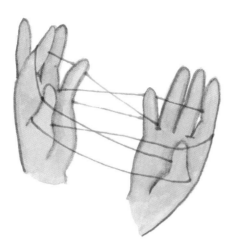

5. Bend your thumbs over the thumb strings *farther* from you and under the *closer* index finger strings. Pull tight.
6. Bend your pinkies over the pinkie strings *closer* to you and under the *farther* away index finger strings. Pull tight again.

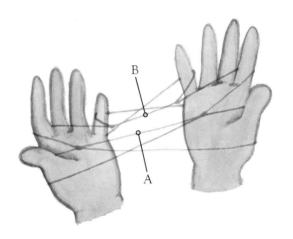

7. Here's the part where having a friend is handy. Ask your friend to take the *lower* string on each thumb and pinkie finger, and pull it up and off of each finger, letting it go loose—but without pulling the top strings off each finger! Pull tight again.
8. Have your friend pull string A over your pinkies, and string B over your thumbs. Pull tight again.

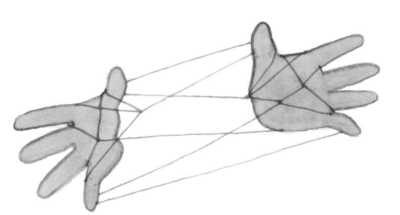

9. Just like in step 7, have your friend take the *lower* string on each thumb and pinkie finger, and pull it up and off of each finger, letting it go loose—but without pulling the top strings off each finger. Pull tight again.

10. Ta-dah! You've made a turtle!